GW01418804

salmonpoetry

*Publishing Irish & International
Poetry Since 1981*

Do Not Touch

SANDRA ANN WINTERS

This collection is published in 2020 by
Salmon Poetry, Cliffs of Moher, County Clare, Ireland
www.salmonpoetry.com   email: info@salmonpoetry.com

Copyright © Sandra Ann Winters, 2020

ISBN 978-1-912561-80-3

Cover & Title Page Image: © *Neil Harrison | Dreamstime.com*
Cover Design & Typesetting: *Siobhán Hutson*
Printed in Ireland by Sprint Print

for Steven, Jamie, and Gavin

Acknowledgments

Grateful acknowledgement is made to the editors and judges of the following publications and contests in which these poems appeared or were commended.

Fish Poetry Prize 2019:
  "Anthurium" (long-listed)
  "Do Not Touch" (long-listed)

Flying South 2017:
  "Preachan, Ennistyman, Ireland" published

Flying South 2018:
  "Under the Moon" published and also nominated for the 2019 Pushcart Prize by the editors of *Flying South*

Randall Jarrell Poetry Competition 2017:
  "Under the Moon" (Honorable Mention)

Randall Jarrell Poetry Competition 2019:
  "Atlanta Braves" (Honorable Mention)

W. B. Yeats Society of N. Y; 2019 Yeats Poetry Prize:
  "Our Irish Garden" ("Noted with Pleasure")

Special thanks to Janet Joyner for her wise guidance, to Jessie Lendennie for bringing this book forth, and to Siobhán Hutson for her skillful and artistic book design.

Contents

I

II

I

Anthurium

*This is the talk of the flower, the truth of the blossom:
the glory of eternal life is fully shining here.*

ZENKEI SHIBAYAMA

Flamingo Lily
layers of moist pink spathes
inflorescence in folds, flaring out
from the base of the fleshy spike
where tiny flowers, jewels, grow
like the enchantress, painted tongue,
poisonous beauty, come here.

Do Not Touch

You ran your fingers around the stones of the ice house
that stored salmon caught in the Blackwater.
You pulled the Mont Freesia to your face, smelled the blossoms.
In Kilkenny castle you brushed your hands over the antique table,
pressed the silk wallpaper, a rich embossed green,
picked up a silver knife from the place setting, felt its heft.
Hands on the glass cabinet as if you could reach into the past,
you studied a photo. *Gosh isn't that amazing,* you said.
In Saint Canice's Cathedral, you traced the circle
of the medieval font, dipped your hands in the holy water,
stroked the marble effigy of Margaret Butler,
caressed her closed eyes, her cheeks, her hair,
a slight smile on her lips, as if she were your lover,
her hands folded in prayer. And then you touched me.

Our Irish Garden

You weed the garden, a microcosm,
shelter the magenta hydrangea blossoms,
weave wisteria through the trellis,
the fragrant vine always zealous,
clip the bay laurel to save the blueberries.
You gather crabapples to make jellies,
prune the rosemary to garnish the lamb,
cut the sage to cook with marjoram,
gather the nasturtiums for salads,
trim the heather, save a chrysalis.
In the moist soil, the slugs take their chances
when you fertilize, manure and ashes.
You comfort me against the setting sun,
my seedsman, you blow a kiss on the run.

Enough Said

Under the leafy branches, spoonfuls of light,
we said enough to make you want to stay the afternoon.
Your feet touched my red-painted toes to my delight,
your hands covered my breasts, under the sun,
the tangle of our legs made me spin and spin.
I stroked your spine with my palms, nothing we had planned.
The birds in the shadows witnessed not our sin
but our grassy bed and how the oak spans.
Our love was hot—we pulled apart, smiled.
We were not in a hurry, but old and wild.

I like something about just sleeping with a man in the dark

back to back, butts bare, round hips against his bottom,
the warmth of the body, all soft valleys and hills, the sounds
    of light snores,
the smells of sweat and salt, the palms of feet rubbing.

At dawn I turn to face him, our bodies curling.
The long sleep over, I rub his face, cheeks, eyes, his lips.
I weave my fingers through his curly chest. He soothes the
    seam along my spine.

Later I go separately to my day of classes.
I ask my students to read *Waiting For Godot*. In a circle they go.
We always find something, hey Didi, to give us the impressions we exist.

I Never Slept with a Woman with Red-Painted Toes

Your feet stroke the tops of my mine,
across the bones of my thin skin.
You slide your feet up my shins.

The slave girl took Queen Nefertiti's feet
washed them in sea water,
kneaded them with the sun's heat.
She cleaned the sand between the toes
slid the warm stones up the Queen's thighs.

Love's pulses leap. You hold my hands
along your loins, my head upon your chest,
you marvel at that crimson.

She mixed mud and the sea,
shined her legs like white breasts,
blended the gum arabic, egg whites,
beeswax, varnishes, lacquers,
ruby red fit for a Queen as I am for you.

The Way She Is

If you love her in bed, the way she moves,
then you must love the way she holds the hoe.
You must love the way she stirs the soup
and rocks the children in the cradle.
You must love the way she combs her hair
and holds a book.

If you rub her softness as she lies on top of you,
then you must tie her apron around that softness.
You must love the way she washes a cup,
soap and water sliding off the china,
the way she sways with a broom,
sings a tune.

If you love the wetness when she comes
then you must love the way she peels an orange,
a little juice seeping down her chin,
the way she watches the full moon slip
behind the trees. If you must slide your tongue
between her lips, then you must love her in the sun.

I love

the way the *l* leans
into the *o,* the *v* and *e.*
I love you friend
who reads poetry
to me when I lie
on the sofa with fever.
I love Liam the waiter
who takes breaks
from drawing Guinness
to talk about
the rain and the game.
I love you dear cabbie
who chats
about the myths
of Ireland,
the Children of Lir
transformed into swans.
I love you goldfinch,
who lands at
my feeder outside
the window,
brilliant yellow
with a conical bill,
the cadence of your call.

Lament for a Husband

The copper kettle whistles.
I gather peppermint for the tea,
warm the cup, add sugar and cream,
carry the saucer to the parlor, faithfully.

He naps in the chair,
snores softly, a small devotion,
his hands across his knees.
He dreams of shaping trees.

He counts the wood he must chop,
building the shelves in his shop,
marks the rails he will cut for the porch,
wooden spindles made of birch.

I catch the movement of his eyes,
offer the steaming cup of tea.
He reaches not for the cup, but for me,
a quick peck on the cheek.

I laugh, and then cry,
he touches me with a farewell.
His duty to love a wife, is not in his heart.
He desires to go, to be apart.

To travel afar, sleep in a tent,
see the clouds below the ascent,
watch the eagle flying on high.
He sips the tea with a sigh.

Daybreak

I wake to the sounds of the old crank grinding
the English mill screwed to the farmhouse table,
his arm goes round and round, hand on the oak handle.
Beans go round and round between the blades
into a black cup. He sifts the coffee
into a French press. I hear the kettle whistle,
his own tune as he sings *All of Me.*
I smell the fresh brew.
Hope his love is grounded.

The Spirit Level

I remember the handsaw as you built birdfeeders
out of tigerwood and cedar to teach the children a skill.
Then there was the bird you saved from the door,
a finch, beak caught in the screen,
your roughened hands holding that flash of gold.
You did not fret, a man of few words, but a strong grip.
You were gentle, as you medicated,
sutured our son's cut foot, a calm doctor.

I see the lemon tree you grew from seed,
the tartness in a tart. I see the trees
you planted, grown now to the canopy.
They sway in the wind catch the bird songs,
sounds from breezy afternoons where I nap
on the screened porch you fashioned. You painted
the ceiling blue and one-hundred-fifty rails just for me.
You renovated and innovated, and crafted a husband.

Day and Night

All in stipple upon trout that swim.

GERARD MANLEY HOPKINS

We sat in the dark, drinking Cabernet.
Frogs croaked in the night
like the horn on the ferry that took
us to Bear Island, a sandy beach.
The candlelight stippled the fish in the pond.
Angelfish sought the water striders floating
on the surface, honeysuckle, a fragrant thought.

When the morning rose the day was a song.
We ate toast and honey under the sun.
You hung the white starched linens,
pegs guarding against the wind,
the early melody of blowing clothes,
tarragon in the strawberry pot, profusion.
But the day was not the night.

A Luminous Strike

We walk the wooden path to the strand,
step into the white sand. The low tide
tempts us closer, our feet covered
by sea foam, algae blooms, all across the dunes.

The breeze blows beneath vast clouds;
love is slippery as a fish, but our hearts grow
from the salty storm. You lay your arm low
around my sandy waist and lead the way.

After sunset a thin streak of blue lines the shore,
flaxen lightning cracks in a sable sky.
Polaris points to the plough, waves crest,
moist air seduces us.

Hat in the Wind

The wind took your hat,
whisked high above the street,
it whizzed over the speeding cars,
and turned up the sidewalk.
You caught it just as it tugged again.

I'd like to have a girlfriend,
but girlfriends are hard to find.

You, the hat man, and I talked
about mothers and long-gone noble brothers.
We talked about poetry. You quoted,
the irrepressible spirit, I knew,
listened, I understood the price.

I caught each word so slow and easy.
You caught the hat, but we flew away.

An Imagined Life

We will live in an Irish stone cottage by the Lee,
grow cabbages, carrots, parsley and thyme.
We will each have a desk, shelves full of books,
a bed, by the window out which to look.
We will rest in the noon sun to read and write.
Our poems will be composed in the Irish light.
I will make slow simmering potato soup.
We will waltz on the kitchen tiles to *All of Me,*
hold hands on long evening walks in the mist.
You will read me John Clare. You will laugh at my saying,
Dear I would have liked to have made love to Shakespeare.
I will come to your bed, sometimes on fire, other nights,
a candle's soft glow. In the morning, I will reach for my diary.
You will bring me elderflower tea and reach for me.

The Imprint

The pillow is a little askew to the right,
the roundness of your head, as you slept on your
side facing away. In the pitch dark room,
I knew you were there. I could hear you breathing,
slight puffs. You left the scent of sweat, salty.
Now, I trace the places where your shoulders lay,
where your ribs pressed on Jasmine white sheets.
I wanted to sleep where you had lain,
but didn't want to change where
all that was left were the creases.

Falling for You

Beds in the Hilton Hotel,
pushed together, not attached,
you came to me
in the curtained–darkened room,
just a slight sliver of light, enough
to see your eyes, green for me
from country places, but here now.
You pushed my arms, not away, but closer,
Lovely, lovely you said, but I knew you meant
not love at all, just the feel of it.
You pulled me to your twin bed to relax,
but the beds rolled apart,
and we fell through the crack.

Just Not Quite There Until...

We went through the buffet, lifted the chafing dish lids,
sat through our breakfast, weeping tomatoes, mushrooms,
white and black pudding. We ate and talked
of a complacent day's work at editing—
corrections, condensations and modifications,
commented on the clematis outside the restaurant window,
the lemon tree not bearing, the rain water plunging
into a stagnant pool, over river stones, the fuchsia,
dancing ballerinas. It was an ordinary morning
until I brushed a crumb from your cheek.

The Outing

Friends, poets, we walked the path of Torc falls,
around the lakes of Killarney to the Weir.
We stopped to hear the seagulls' calls.
You asked if I would like a drive to Inch Beach,
told me the story of Brian Boru, reached
for my hand. We ate cabbage and beef in our hotel,
breathed in the sea, heard the ocean swell.
We talked about poetry and poets, Dylan Thomas wrote
I can always feel your heart. Dance tunes are always right.
And we did dance, crashed a wedding delight,
waltzed, closer now than friends.
You walked to my room, kissed me,
waited, but I didn't turn the key.

The Law of Attraction

The courtship of these dazzling
acrobats, a liquid summer day, fringes of a pond,
diving, twirling, flashing, as he chases her
wispy wings, brilliant green, hover over.
He darts forward, turns back, weaves in the wind,
dips and snatches any female in his path
while she, unaware, warms in the sun.
He is a thief and attacks, pulling and biting.
She outmaneuvers him, zigzagging, spiraling
upward or downward, skimming on water, fleeing.
A buzz in the air, a clash, add a blue flash.
He catches her, blazing, transparent.

Footsteps

After W. B. Yeats

There are things we don't tread on; clumps of moss,
worms wriggling through the earth, flowers in the field,
the off-note singing of a best friend, the high notes
of *The Marriage of Figaro,* a shantung beige dress,
the silver hair of a woman, her pink-painted toes.
We don't tread on the moon, standing stones,
the village funeral hearse followed by walkers
under umbrellas, flaming candles in the cathedral,
prayers we whisper in the light of church windows.
We don't tread on kisses or dreams,
what makes a thing beautiful.

I Am Learning You

On our way, you check the gearshift twice,
and pull over for others to pass.
When we end our daily journey,
I watch you eat your cabbage and ham,
working your way neatly across your plate.
On evening strolls you go ahead, deliberate,
to point to the Spring Gentian,
small blue surprises between the stones.
I feel safe with you, walking across the Burren,
lying in the night with your heart on my own.

Reign in My Heart

You held my hand as we sat on the sofa,
curved to each other, speaking softly
of books, *Beckett's Friendship,*
Rilke's *Crowned With Dreams*
of poems, Heaney's *Blackberry-Picking*
You ate that first one and its flesh was sweet—
like thickened wine: summer's blood was in it,
of a mother who passed on a full-moon night,
of sons who walked and climbed the Reeks
and fathers who for the sheep put out the grain.
We whispered into the early daylight.
I wanted to hold you tightly,
but you would have turned away
like a flower in the rain.

Dragonfly I

In the evening he seeks midges
with a hyper-thrust mechanism,
ejects water, a jet-propelled system.
Making a meal of what he pleases,
he darts in a speed-boost,
turns on a dime, hovers in place,
flies backwards, catches on the fly,
gleans stems, snatches mosquitoes
perched on lotus leaves;
faster than my eyes can follow
and my heart can beat.

Dragonfly II

At dusk to escape from the summer heat,
I slip naked into my Koi pond,
brush against the lily pads,
round, radial leaves, mucilage slick.
I see you up close on the water flower,
a bit of cobalt floating on a tip of yellow,
your eyes, green gemstones pop on a papery mask.
You speed away, lacy wings steering tight turns.
In a glimmer you are gone.

Four Nights to Remember

We are shy as we ask for a double room.
She raises her brows, but takes our fee,
says coffee and tea are complimentary. I am unsure,
after so many years. Has it been ten?
Not to worry. It will be all right if we both are relaxed.
Well, I am climaxed, most daring act of my life.
You touch my breasts. You kiss me.
No speaking. What would we say?
You slide your hands over my ample thighs.
We are not meek. In the dark I hold you tightly.
At the train station, you turn once to wave good-bye.

A Room with a Sea View

We are folded like origami, shins, thighs, pelvis,
sweat and soft screams in the day-lit room.
Your touch, all teeth and tongue,
I run my fingers over your forehead, eyelids,
stroke your feathered chest. Nice you say.
You come to bed in nothing but a T-shirt.
I pull it off laughing. You say, *does this make it better?*
Rolling over each other we exchange places.
All through the morning and the afternoon's sun
we warm; windows tilted toward the harbor.

Regret

After Yeats

I should have been easy
while you traced circles
around my belly, up my breastbone.

I should have felt your fingers in my hair.
I should have heard your whispers,
nothing to fear.

I should have listened closer to the myths,
Deirdre of the sorrows, Niamh and Oisin,
should have understood.

I should have read your poetry,
gotten to the core
seen the metaphors.

I should have caught the look of your eyes,
the shadows deepening,

Snow Ballerinas

cerulean skies
cranes dance around each other
yellow bills desire

red coronets flame
black tertial feathers
over white tails

ritual ballet
foreplay's choreography
coupling splendor

The Night Was Dark

We coiled, arms and legs
like the vines of a wreath.
I joked. *Could We Be Any Closer?*
You massaged each of my vertebrae.
I stretched your arms up, along the pillow,
our fingers braided, palms moist,
kissed your cheeks, whispered,
Let's be together always, never let go.
As you left, I stood seducing a smile,
but your last goodbye was silence.
The day was clear.

Flying Flowers

He dances in the air, a prelude,
searching and perching for a Swallowtail,
delicate rhythms, circling, leading,
she will follow in *The Kiss Waltz*.
A courting pair of sulphurs
spiraling upward into the sky.
The semen enters a small pouch
inside the female's abdomen.
She carries this pouch of spermatozoa and eggs,
lays a few on Queen Anne's lace,
Milkweed, Goldenrod, Dutchman's Pipe.
He will try to entice females many times;
she will mate only once to her pleasure.

Rejection

In bed we hear the drum from O'Kelly's.
We rock to the beat, locked in a kiss.
Your hands caress my breasts, ease down my belly.
Our words, liquid, slide between us in the darkness.

I gave her up. I tried and tried,
but the depression got to me.
You're not the only one who knows love refused.
I pull you to me, hold your sadness, my own slips away.

In the Dew-falling Hours

You read poetry to me
then kiss me long and deeply.
This is what love remembers.
Sometimes I stare at your photo
and play Bach's Musikalisches Opfer
just to believe that you exist.
Barn owls, when their mate dies,
mourn for seasons.
Cheetahs howl for cubs
devoured by lions,
but do not question *Why?*

At Dusk

Today I dissolved the yeast into flour,
kneaded until smooth, punched
the dough down and waited
for a golden brown. I thought
about the grocery list, the avocados,
the Clementines, about planting
the mint and thyme near the rue.
Today I drank blackberry wine
under the branches of the willow tree,
watched the Koi as they glowed
and waited for the closing of the lilies.
Today, not once, did I think of you.

II

Wintering

*Lavender to be a thing of great value, especiall good
for all griefes and paines.*

ST. MARK

Violet whorls of lavender lean to sunlight
streaming through the glass, held by pale
blue mullions in sliding sash windows.
Stalks hold seven flowers like fairy thimbles.
The priest prepared the holy essences.
The Syrians called it Nard, a thing of great value.
I snip the sweet blossoms to float in my bath,
fragrant oils warm my chilled heart.

Fishing

I

I touch your maple box of ashes
every time I pass you, Father.
Eighteen years you have been
on top of the old piano.
Sometimes I light a candle,
sit at the bench and play
Red Sails In the Sunset, the lines you sang
Carry My Loved One Home Safely to Me.

II

A vase of wild blue chicory sits next
to you, your favorite,
the color of your eyes.
I remember our wildflower afternoons
pushing tall grasses aside,
Queen Anne's Lace, Asters,
Scarlet Bergamot, Foxglove,
Bluebells. You cut each flower
with your penknife,
taught me the names,
how to find the hidden blooms.

III

I remember your rolled trousers,
white froth circling your ankles,
a thin line tugging in the sea,
the flatfish flipping between your toes.

You held her, wet and sticky,
her eye once, migrated,
both now facing you.
The golden flounder
granted you a wish
as the poor fisherman
in the tale, but you did not command
the sun, the moon and the heavens.

IV

We fished on the dock at dusk,
you baited my hook,
blood-red worms stained your hands.
Casting, we struck a school of crappie
or was it sunfish, specks, sac-a-lait?
Tin buckets brimmed with half-pounders,
I gutted for dinner, scales flew
from the sharp snap of a tablespoon.

V

Then your hair grayed and you retired,
stocked your back-yard pond,
surrounded by sunflowers, with catfish.
You fed them, an easy catch
for your six-year-old grandson.
The big white fish caught,
you easily released it again and again
until you freed her for all summers to come.

Under the Moon

My daddy built the out-of-house for us,
whitewashed the walls, cut a star in the door.
He pasted the poem "Cremation of Sam McGee"
on the wall. Stubs of candles lay in a cubby
and of course, always the bucket of lime.
I could see the moon through the star cutout,
and knew I was lucky.

The night skies followed me to the sleeping porch
where I lay awake in the cooler southern air.
That cold, dry globe, studded with craters,
and strewn with rocks and dust led me through
my periodic rises and falls. I pondered
the full, the waning, gibbous,
the waxing crescent moons.

The moon has followed me all my nights,
sleeping on the hard earth
under the Sierra and Utah skies,
through nights on the sand dunes by the Atlantic.
It has followed me rocking on the glider
that stretches out on the screened porch.

When I pee to the glinting stars' tune,
I know my daddy was the man-in-the-moon.

Scars

First child, she held me warm against her breast,
a child herself. She combed my curls, tied them with a bow.
For birthday gifts she made us fudge,
wrapped a shoebox in blue, star-covered paper,
added an orange, a special treat.

One Saturday, she threw the wet washcloth
over the Chrysler, scrubbed the windows,
then she slipped on the soapy trunk
onto the sharp license plate,
cut her knee, deep enough for stitches.

Today we will make meringues for Gerald in Korea.
Cut the Queen Anne's lace, the blue chicory.
Bring a jar for the bouquet. It's Friday, your father
will rake oysters for stew. I'll make a bread pudding
from the breakfast biscuits.

She loved the four of us. In the spring she lost her youngest.
She held the loss in her heart, never forgot
there were four of us, not less one.
Today when I hold my ninety-year-old-mother,
I see that scar, a tiny blooming flower.

Atlanta Braves

The moon was full the night you died.
I could see it though the bedroom window,
glossed gold, glazing the dark room with light,
close to the earth, bright, a Supermoon.

I kissed your hands, large now against your shrunken body,
climbed in beside you, held you in my arms,
a wet sponge on your lips, tiny drops of water
squeezed into your thirsty mouth, dry and cracked.

I slept on the floor beside your bed to catch you
from falling out. The hard floor did not bend to my curves.
I could hear your quiet breath. Often I heard it stop,
rose to check on you and whispered, *Mother.*

You cried a long night, *Help me, Help me.*
I sang your favorite song, "Take Me Out to the Ballgame."
You calmed to hear me, your daughter.
Then the moon called you away.

Roaring Water Bay

He roasts peppers until tender,
pours hot water over the red bells,
plunges them into a cooling rinse.
Skins slip off. Seeds flake
to the bowl beneath, become supper.

Outside the island's rugged pulse beats
against the rocks, not tender at all,
but necessary. Seals sing in the roiling water.
The willow fence woven with roses
arches firm to the cliff.

He serves the soup,
The sea is pure horizon.

Sherkin Island

We leave the ferryman, walk the path.
Stone-stacked walls fill the horizon.
Trailing honeysuckles rove through hedgerows.
Hart's Tongue grows. Marsh orchids bow.
I pick Lady's Bed Straw. You eat sloes.
Black-backed gulls, terns, choughs
drift on the wind. Puffins cling to a cliff.
We watch harbor seals roil in the waves.
Clashing rocks and islands, sea cliffs,
lavender shallows, green-blue white caps—
these are the islands of the dolphin.
On the strand, I collect oyster shells,
turn them over, look for the silver shine.
Over and over again, we are one.

Pearl to Pearl

I found it
while eating a wild oyster.
I could barely cradle it,
an iridescent irritant,
tiny treasure. I palmed it
in my hand, let it roll.

Pearls on the hemisphere-
shaped maple, hold
onto ferny leaves
—those hands of frogs—
as the branches
tip across the horizon.

Two pearls, birthed
from a wet morning.

Pares, Pears, and Pairs

for Kathy O'Connor

She was born into Laethanta na Bó Riabhaiche, the days
of the brindled cow grazing in the harsh spring weather,
the end of "Old March." Fodder scarce,
the foxy heifer, sienna freckled with fawn grey, survives.

Pears sear in sugary syrup seasoned with slivers of ginger.
She shall serve them for lunch. Sons and daughters
will taste the sweet flesh of the fruit as she raises
a red glass to toast children leaving home.

Pears slide down her fingers, along the brush
onto the wet paper, alizarin crimson, windsor green,
round-bottomed like two women, fleshy hips sitting
on a varnished sheet, bent to each other.

She tastes colors, holds them in her palms,
turns them round for us to see while we listen
to the green glaze of her music. Then she lies down to sleep
like a rain-covered road, winding through gilded gorse.

From the Mother's Voice

for Deirdre

I sat on my nursing home bed in my gray wool best,
legs swollen, stretched out like two plump courgettes.
You poured champagne into Waterford Crystal.
I toasted us, *sláinte*. You came to me
with bags full of books, big-print mysteries
from the Kanturk library. You told me, daughter,
about your days, gathering frogspawn for the children
to watch fat specks burst into tadpoles and about
climbing Caherbarnagh with your friends,
sharing hot parsnip soup on the peak. You folded my new,
slim wheelchair, brought me out for lamb and roast potatoes,
a linen tablecloth. Some days I wanted to rock you in my arms.
Your eyes red, I knew you'd had to gather up the horizon
and move it once again. You lifted a straw to my mouth,
a little bird chirping for a drop, a water-offering prayer.
I waited through the wind, rain and sun,
through the rhythm of my days. I waited for your blue eyes.

Sister

The older I get, the closer I move to my roots
those growing up days, working my way
through university carrying food trays
to hungry and rude folks, another spoon,
but my potatoes are overdone; I am always on the run,
on and on further back to my elocution classes
pronouncing my t's and p's unlike the masses.
Was it yesterday I was twisting and shouting,
running around Susie because *Sugar Pie, Honey Bunch,*
I couldn't help myself? After *Go Devils Go!*
In sweltering summers lying in the hammock
reading Daphne du Maurier, swinging my foot,
hop-scotch on the sidewalk with white chalk
Red Rover, Red Rover, send Sybil right over.
On Saturday nights in the large tin tub
our mother lathering white Ivory Soap
over our backs, the sense of her scrub,
we shivered into the woodstove-heated towels,
then back to lying with you sister under the pines,
which were covered in Virginia Creeper vines.

Pillowcases

My grandmother embroidered
Sweet Dreams and *Good Night*
on pillowcases that I have kept since her death,
fifty years ago. When I was unhappy,
alone, I slept on those pillowcases.
They comforted me, kept me alive.
Today *Sweet Dreams* tore in half,
and I cannot find *Good Night*.
What happens when we lose
the past, as when the cupboard fell
and all great-grandmother's
china broke into trifling pieces
as if she had never lived?

Canning Tomatoes

Mother bends
like *The Gleaners*
gathering Purple Cherokees,
Brandywines, Early Girls,
hands them to grandmother,
to add to the basket
of vine-ripened treasures.
Tempted, we eat a few
hot from the sun,
red juice dripping from our chins.

Late in the evening
we come to the canning,
dip the tomatoes in
the great blue-speckled pot
of boiling water,
wait for the skins to crack
like grandmother's hands.
We cut the fruit into cold Mason jars,
add salt and lemon juice,
the flats and rims.

Tomatoes simmer for fifty minutes
while we scrub down
the nine-foot maple table
to the marrow. We change aprons,
rock in the kitchen chairs,
talk quietly into the midnight hours,
about losing old friends,
the gathering of the church flowers.

Lifting the hot jars
in a cloud of steam,
we set them on old towels to cool,
wait for the pop of the flats, the seal,
count, proudly fifty-three jars
ready for snowy days.
We scrub our hands
from the blood-red stains.

Frying Fish

At seven my son cleans the stalls,
dung clings to his boots
onto our old kitchen floor.
He cooks his breakfast,
frying fish.
It's brain
food Mom.
I have a test today.
At sixteen he moves
to the stable tack room
like Apache desert dwellers,
who built a separate teepee
for their teenage boys.
I wait for him
to come home,
but he swims
away as the salmon
in the stream.

There is an Edge to Our Love

Mom, watch the curb. Walking ahead,
my black purse swinging from his shoulder,
he talks me over the broken pavement.
I had held his hand across the street once.
Now he forges on with cautions tossed,
Watch the dog, wait for the light, go slow.
I am broken now like the pavement. He is not
trying to piece me together, but to get me there.
We do get to the theater. He puts me in a recliner
pushes the buttons, I swing back,
my popcorn flying. He picks it up,
puts it in a napkin for me to hold.
I asked you not to tell David about the car, he snaps.
I wish you wouldn't, and if I want to buy a black BMW I will.
Back to the street, he walks ahead, my black purse still swinging.
Watch the ledge, Mom.

Ennistymon, Ireland

I have reasons to watch the crows
outside my hotel window.
I watch father feeding mother
as she rests over the river.
He brings her nuts and bees;
she protects their young.
Together they teach the predators are owls.
I taught you young son about the perils,
diving deep in the pond, playing in the street,
sledding on a lake. I watch the crows,
the comfort of feeding
eight fleshy necks stretching.
Crows fly, flapping wings, rarely a glide,
but you do glide, son
skydiving, kayaking down the Potomac.
I sit here alone, have reasons
for watching crows outside my window
who form shadows against the evening sun.

Do Not Touch is SANDRA ANN WINTERS' second book of poems from Salmon Poetry. Her previous publications were *The Place Where I Left You* (Salmon Poetry) and a chapbook *Calving Under the Moon* (Finishing Line Press). Her poems have appeared in journals and anthologies including the *Cork Literary Review, Southword, the North Carolina Literary Review, Flying South, Even the Daybreak: 35 Years of Salmon Poetry, The Deep Heart's Core: Irish Poets Revisit a Touchstone Poem,* and others. She is the winner of the 2011 Gregory O'Donoghue International Poetry Competition, and a Pushcart nominee twice. Her poems have received a variety of awards and recognition, including most recently commendation by the 2019 Yeats Poetry Prize (W. B. Yeats Society of NY). She was a professor of Irish and English literature for 30 years at Guilford College in Greensboro, NC.

salmonpoetry

Cliffs of Moher, County Clare, Ireland

"Like the sea-run Steelhead salmon that thrashes upstream to its spawning ground, then instead of dying, returns to the sea— Salmon Poetry Press brings precious cargo to both Ireland and America in the poetry it publishes, then carries that select work to its readership against incalculable odds."

TESS GALLAGHER

The Salmon Bookshop
& Literary Centre

Ennistymon, County Clare, Ireland

"Another wonderful Clare outlet."
The Irish Times, 35 Best Independent Bookshops